The Dare to Be Seen Journal

A companion workbook to boost your confidence and stage presence

Elisa Di Napoli

EDN Publishing

Contents

DOWNLOAD the Dare to Be Seen BONUS PACKAGE

including a

FREE AUDIOBOOK and ONLINE COURSE

Templates, Training, Hypnosis Sessions and Resources to Kickstart your Journey into Authentic Confidence under the Spotlight!

TO DOWNLOAD GO TO

https://elisadinapoli.com/bonuses

Scan with your camera phone

1

INTRODUCTION

HOW TO USE YOUR DARE TO BE SEEN JOURNAL

Welcome! Congratulations on beginning the process of investing time and energy to document the journey of transformation you are about to embark upon with the *Dare to Be Seen* Journal. The following is a quick overview of how to use this journal to maximise its benefits and your results.

The journal is designed as a companion to the book and online course "Dare to Be Seen: from stage fright to stage presence". While both the book and the online course can be used on their own, the journal will help you capitalise on your significant lessons and accomplishments by keeping you accountable and focused so you can review your progress, deepen your understanding and cement your learning through practical and reflective coaching exercises.

While the book explores the theory and structure behind the method that will help you overcome stage nerves, the online course provides you with pre-recorded hypnotic sessions you can listen to from the comfort of your home, so you don't have to record your own. The journal is the final piece of the puzzle that will guide you through each session, so you can document, reflect and complete all coaching exercises in one place.

The journal also makes it easier for you to create your own hypnotic sessions should you wish to do so, by guiding you through the essential practical steps needed to create and use your own suggestions with self-hypnosis, so you don't have to go back to the book to dig out the information you need.

Each chapter includes questions for you to reflect on, with space to write on the page, as well as various ways of keeping track of your progress. A quick summary of the book's or course's most important content is also given, so you can draw from its essential principles and put them into practice to get the results you want faster.

There are many life-enhancing benefits of using the Dare to Be Seen Journal, some of which include:

GAINING CLARITY: The process of writing down your thoughts forces you to think through them enough to understand them. Thus, The Dare to Be Seen journal will give you more clarity, allowing you to brainstorm, and helping you to achieve your performance and confidence goals and more effectively work through your problems and challenges.

CAPTURING IDEAS: Journaling helps you not only expand your ideas, but also prevents you from losing the important ideas that you may want to act on in the future.

REVIEWING SESSIONS: The Dare to Be Seen journal enables you to review and strengthen all of the lessons you're learning.

ACKNOWLEDGING YOUR PROGRESS: Going back and re-reading your Dare to Be Seen journal entries and seeing how much progress you've made is one of the most empowering, confidence-inspiring and enjoyable experiences that can't really be duplicated any other way.

The Dare to Be Seen journal allows you to document your journey to creating the most confidence you've ever imagined having on stage... Starting right NOW.

2

DIY Anyone?

Steps to Self-Hypnosis

If you have decided to hypnotise yourself rather than take advantage of the pre-recorded sessions included in the online course "Dare to Be Seen", read on.

In this chapter I will provide you with a brief recap of the different stages of a typical hypnotic session, as well as a summary of the conditions needed to hypnotise yourself. I will also include scripts for you to follow in order to create your own session.

First of all, let's take a brief look at how to effectively hypnotise yourself.

A typical session consists of four stages, namely:

1. Induction
2. Deepening
3. Suggestions (or if a hypnotherapist is guiding you, many other techniques)
4. Awakening

Hypnosis is created during the induction when the subject is induced into a light hypnotic state followed by the deepening which is the time when a deeper state of hypnosis is reached. After the deepening phase comes the interesting part. If you are going to hypnotise yourself, suggestions will be used in this part of the session.

After the 'meat and potatoes' part of the session is over, it will be time to get back to normal conscious awareness so you can transition smoothly to everyday external reality. If you want to hypnotise yourself you need to follow the above structure. I shall include an example of a full induction and deepening as well as the standard awakening procedure below. However, feel free to use your own if you prefer.

Another method of self-hypnosis is to guide yourself without a formal induction. If you have been to a self-hypnosis class, you will know how to do this. If you choose to use this method, I would recommend recording a 5 to 10-minute gap at the beginning of your recordings before you begin your suggestions (please refer to Chapter 6 of the main book for more in depth explanations).

You have three options:

1. you could record your own induction, suggestions and awakening.
2. you could leave a 5- 10 minute gap at the beginning of your recording and then record your own suggestions and awakening.
3. you could listen to the pre-recorded hypnotic sessions provided for you on the online course Dare to Be Seen.

My choice is

....

....

....

How to induce hypnosis

Before you start, please be aware that if you are using self-hypnosis recordings at night—unless you are quite anxious and find it hard to relax—it is better not to listen to them in bed, or you may fall asleep. Instead, sit on a comfortable chair with your back and neck straight. If the tendency is to let your head drop down, don't let it; you don't want to be drowsy and you may give yourself a stiff neck otherwise. Don't slouch either. Instead, try to get the support you need.

You can use meditation cushions if you are a meditator and it feels familiar and comfortable to you. If you are sitting on a chair or lying down, make sure you keep your feet flat on the floor and your legs and arms uncrossed. Always use the same position so your body will learn to associate the posture with self-hypnosis.

Whether you are listening to your recording at night, early in the morning, or during a break in the day, make sure you switch off your mobile notifications, close social media, and avoid all distractions by putting your phone on airplane mode. You could put a sign on the door so you are not interrupted and if there are sounds around you, tell yourself you are going to ignore them, as if they came from a TV playing in another room with the volume turned down. Imagine they are a background soundtrack to your relaxation, helping you zone in on your inner world.

Step 1: Adopt the hypnotic mindset

In order to access hypnosis, you need to adopt the 'hypnotic mindset'. These are its essential elements:

- Expect success
- Have a positive attitude
- Trust yourself to be receptive
- Watch your language
- Pretend it is working until it does

When you are ready to record the induction, remember to use a gentle and assured tone. Be encouraging and take it slow. Resist the urge to rush; instead, feel each word, and as you speak into your recording device, imagine how long it would take for you to respond to your suggestions. Be absorbed in the process. When you listen to the recording, trust you are doing this the way that is right for you. Being as still as possible will enable you to be more focused on the hypnotic process.

Step 2: Breathing exercise

Once you have assumed your chosen position, take a deep breath through your nose. Count to 4 on the inhale, hold the breath for the count of 4, exhale out for the count of 4, and again hold the breath for 4.

Each time you inhale, imagine calm entering your body and spreading through every muscle and nerve. As you exhale, imagine letting go of any stress or tension. If you like, imagine a colour you associate with calmness spreading through your body every time you breathe in. As you breathe out, imagine letting go of any tension like water flowing down the drain, and being released out of your body through your feet and fingertips. Use your imagination to change this any way it works for you. Repeat six times or as long as you need to feel the calming effect of this kind of breathing.

Step 3: The induction

The following can be used as a script. Record it word for word or add your own flavour to it.

Eye fixation

Without moving from your position, imagine looking at a real or imagined spot located as high as possible in front of you. Keeping your head still, allow your eyeballs to roll up as if you were looking in between your eyebrows. Do not bend your neck or tilt the head; keep it straight. As you fix your eyes in this way, concentrate your attention only on the spot and you will feel your eyes quickly becoming tired.

If your eyelids start fluttering, it's a good sign. Breathe in while keeping your eyes on the spot with your eyeballs rolled up. Breathe out. As you take another breath in imagine that your eyelids are getting heavier. Tell yourself they want to close and imagine how wonderfully comfortable it will be when they do. Breathe out. Keep your gaze fixed without moving at all and again take a third breath in while keeping your eyeballs up.

Imagine you are so tired you are trying to fight sleep but your body wants to drift off.

You are now feeling increasingly relaxed with each breath you take. Remember what it's like to feel so drowsy and sleepy; your eyelids feel heavy and want to close. As soon as your eyes are ready to close let them and as they do, keep your eyeballs up and notice the fluttering sensation in your eyes. Now, drop your chin just a fraction so you get that looking down feeling you would experience if you were looking down a flight of stairs. Then allow your eyeballs to go back to your normal position.

The magnets

You can now show yourself the power of your wonderful imagination. Rub the palms of your hands together really fast until you notice the heat and 'energy' in between them. Hold your hands in front of you with the palms facing each other. Allow them to be about fifteen centimetres apart.

When you are ready, imagine that there are two very powerful magnets placed on each palm, drawing the hands together in an irresistible way. The idea is to allow the magnetic force in between your palms to work its magic as you imagine the force acting on both palms, irresistibly drawing them together.

Remember that you are not moving the palms together in a voluntary way, but you are also not resisting that movement. You are only letting your imagination do that for you by allowing the muscles to respond automatically. Fully engage your imagination and see, feel, and sense that magnetic force pulling your hands together.

Pretend you can feel it happening while saying to yourself internally, "With every breath I take, my hands are irresistibly drawing together, pulled in by the force of the magnets. I can try to stop it, but the harder I try, the more the hands are pulled together. As soon as your hands touch, let them drop into your lap like a dead weight.

The staircase deepener

Now that your hands are in your lap, imagine you are at the top of a beautiful staircase. See what your eyes would see, and hear what your ears would hear, and feel what you would feel as you fully imagine this scene. See and sense the staircase. What does it look like?

Now, as I count down from 10 down to 1, with each number you count, take one step down the staircase, and become sleepier and more comfortable with each step. Take step 10, and as you do feel your feet, see your feet, hear your feet treading each step down.

Every step takes you deeper into hypnosis. The deeper you go, the better you feel, and the better you feel, the deeper you go. Now, take step 9 and as you do, allow yourself to feel how heavy and comfortable you are becoming. Give yourself permission to let go. It is safe to unwind, because you are in complete control.

Now, take step 8 and go deeper. And deeper means going deeper into a deeper awareness of your inner self. So, go deeper, drift deeper, sleep deeper. And sleep just means sleep of the nervous system so you can allow yourself to feel more naturally calm and peaceful than you've ever felt before.

Now, take step 7. And as you tune into your body, feel which parts of your body are feeling the most comfortable and calm. It may be a part that's feeling particularly heavy, or particularly light, or maybe a part that doesn't feel much at all. Like the deeper part of a pond, still in the moonlight, let your mind be focused on my voice, the sound of my voice and the pauses in between the words.

And now, take step 6, and tell yourself every sound, inside or outside the room, any movement, only serves to enhance your experience of relaxation, like a background soundtrack to your comfort, or a TV with the sound turned all the way down. And if any thoughts drift in and out of your consciousness, let them be what they are, and then focus back on my words. It's all part of the process.

Now, take step 5, half way down. Tell yourself you are responding so well, you are so focused, you choose to trust you are doing this in the right way for you today. You are protected, you are safe, you are going deeper and deeper into a wonderful hypnotic sleep. You are so engrossed in the process; you notice all the details of shade and light and you are floating down that staircase like water on oil.

Now, take step 4. Sleep deeper. Go deeper. Drift deeper. Allow yourself to soften your body. Perhaps you see a relaxing colour spread through your body, one muscle at a time. Now, take step 3. And as you do, imagine that colour relaxing you deeply, but only as much as you want to. Imagine what those muscles would look and feel like from the inside if they were loose and limp and relaxed.

Now, take step 2 and it's like you are watching a movie of yourself becoming so engrossed, so at ease, like when you are watching a movie or reading your favourite book and you are so connected with the characters and the story, you are so absolutely absorbed in the experience of being in this wonderful feeling of calm and peace. It's like nothing else in the world matters right now...

And now, take step 1. As you do, it's like you can see yourself from above, watching yourself in this moment. You are so aware of yourself that you can imagine what you look like in the position you are in.

It's like you could float up and you could look down at your body there.

And as you leave the building where your body is in, as you float up and explore and you are going higher and higher, you are going deeper and deeper into hypnosis and you see life going on down there, observing the landscape as you travel higher. Now you start to see the larger land mass and even the coastline, and you see less and less details of the streets below as you float higher and higher through the clouds and beyond the atmosphere until you see the entire planet earth in front of you. You can see the planet in its amazing beauty from here in outer space.

And as you notice the different perspective you have here, you can see the earth and all life within it, and you begin to understand more about yourself and life. You begin to benefit from the wisdom of the universe. You begin to gain insight and perspective from this higher place.

Suggestions and change work

Here, add your own autosuggestions (see Chapter 3 and 5 of this Journal) or or use the techniques and strategies that are outlined in each of the sessions in part II, III, and IV of the book Dare to Be Seen (Audio sessions 1-10).

Exit from hypnosis

Now it's time to come out of hypnosis. As you count from 1 to 5, imagine going up a flight of stairs and with each and every number you count, you become more awake, more aware, and at the count of 5, you are fully awake and aware and back to your normal conscious awareness.

Number 1, easily and gently begin returning to your full conscious awareness. Number 2, more and more awake and aware with each number that I count. Number 3, normal sensations are coming back now, feeling good in mind and body, bringing all the benefits of this session to your everyday life. Number 4, wiggling your toes and your fingers, getting ready to open your eyes. Number 5, eyes open, feeling good mentally, physically, and emotionally.

Once your eyes are open, take your time before you drive a car or operate any machinery. Take it easy, allowing for the transition between hypnosis and normal life to happen at your own pace.

Experiment and Commit!

What time of day suits you best for practicing?

....

....

....

....

How do different times feel? Why?

....

....

....

....

Is sitting down or lying down more effective? Why?

....

....

....

....

If you practiced sitting down: did you use a meditation cushion or a chair?

....

....

....

....

What worked best for you? Why?

....

....

....

....

....

....

How can you make sure you will not be disturbed?

....

....

....

....

....

....

What changes can you make (if any) to make the practice more effective?

....

....

....

....

....

....

....

....

....

....

In this chapter we have looked at how to hypnotise yourself effectively. In the next chapter we will explore how to use a very simple and yet powerful exercise to transform your limiting beliefs into empowering suggestions and affirmations you can incorporate into your practice.

3

YOU EMPOWERING BELIEFS

HOW TO CONSTRUCT EFFECTIVE SUGGESTIONS AND AFFIRMATIONS

In this chapter we are going to explore how to create empowering suggestions and affirmations that you can incorporate into your practice so can transform your self-talk, lift your self-esteem and improve your confidence.

The Six Fundamental Mind Hacks for Achieving Lasting Success

If you want to succeed in anything in life, you need to know how to influence your mind. You need to know how to make your mind do what you want it to do, not what you don't.

Have you ever noticed how we are surrounded by messages like 'Don't drink and drive' 'Don't forget your passport' 'Don't touch the button!' 'Don't eat junk!' And how many times have you have done the very thing you were told not to? Why is that? The answer lies in understanding how the mind processes information.

When you know how to truly influence your mind, you can finally understand how to stick to your plans and get the results you are after! For a detailed explanation of the six fundamental mind hacks, please refer to the book "Dare to Be Seen" Chapter 3. However, here's a quick reminder:

1. *Your Mind Does What it thinks you want it to*
2. *Your Mind Responds to only two things*
3. *Emotion trumps logic*
4. *Repetition is the key to changing beliefs*
5. *What you expect tends to be realised*
6. *Your Mind Loves what is familiar and rejects what is unfamiliar*

The best thing you can do to help yourself overcome performance anxiety is to always keep the above rules in mind. To overcome negative beliefs, self-criticism, and self-doubt, is to improve your self-esteem. When your self-esteem goes up, so does your performance. So, pay attention to your self-talk. What language are you using? What are you expecting? What are you focusing on?

Use your limiting beliefs to create your own empowering beliefs

When you notice negative expectations and negative inner dialogue, stop, and take a breath. Are these beliefs serving you or disempowering you? What are you communicating to your mind? Is this what you want?

Remember that most problems in life stem from adopting the following negative limiting core beliefs:

- you are not good enough.
- you don't belong.
- you can't have what you want.

Sound familiar?

You may have already heard of limiting beliefs, but what exactly are they? They are beliefs that limit your range of self-expression and experience. They are 'stoppers' that halt you in your tracks before you even start. They are disempowering and make you feel helpless. Here are some other common ones:

- I don't have enough money
- I don't have time
- I am talented / pretty / young / slim / smart enough
- People are mean / dangerous / against me

Although you may also share some of these, you will also have beliefs specific to you that stop you from being successful in the performing arena. It is important you address them directly. So, how do you know exactly which ones you have?

Let's find out together!

The fastest way to find out is to ask yourself the following questions:

What stands in the way of my (performing) success?

....

....

....

....

....

....

....

....

....

What's stopping me from achieving what I want in this area?

....

....

....

....

....

....

....

....

....

What do I think I am I not good at when it comes to performing in public?

....

....

....

....

....

....

....

....

....

....

Write down the answers. These are your limiting beliefs around performing. Face your fears and be honest.

Now debunk them!

What you believe shapes your feelings and behaviours. Therefore, it is important to re-shape your beliefs to reflect the kind of experience you want to create in your life. When you have identified your limiting beliefs, it is time to transform them. Start by doubting their validity and debunking them rationally first. Take two of your worst disempowering beliefs and ask yourself:

How is this belief absurd or ridiculous?

Who did I learn this from? Is this person worth modelling in this area?

What will it cost me if I don't let go of this belief?

Once you've created your beliefs, they will shape who you are. So, if you want to be better, you need to change your unhelpful toxic beliefs. The best way to let them go is to transform them into positive, empowering convictions. I will refer to these as affirmations or suggestions. The difference between the two is that affirmations are suggestions you say to yourself aloud or internally without the formal use of hypnosis. If, on the other hand, you decide to record the affirmations, you are effectively using self-hypnosis and I will call them suggestions.

To flip your limiting beliefs into affirmations, you can either follow the process described in Audio Session 2 from the "Dare to Be Seen" Book (Chapter 5 of the Journal – Connecting to heart wisdom), or complete the "Hell vs. Opportunity" exercise described later in this chapter. The difference between these methods is that one is more heart-based and the other is more rational. Both are good and can be used together.

Do affirmations really work?

Some people complain that affirmations don't work. In fact, they say they make them feel worse. This is because if you don't follow some important rules when creating

them, they may indeed produce the opposite effect. There are two kinds of people when it comes to letting suggestions and affirmations in. Some people respond well to absolutely positive statements such as, "I am confident on stage" or "I love performing".

Others however, may well be put off by these kinds of statements and feel they just don't ring true. This will happen especially if you are new to affirmations and you are very used to talking to yourself negatively. If you are this kind of person, avoid writing absolutely positive statements.

Instead, use a 'progressive' style until you see positive results. Progressive affirmations suggest a state that is changing over time. So, for example "I am feeling more and more confident every time I am on stage" is a progressive affirmation.

These are the essential guidelines you should follow:

- Always use the present tense
- Only use positive language (no 'not' or 'don't' or 'won't')
- Be specific
- Emotionalise (use words that suggest strong emotion)
- Exaggerate
- Use progressive language when needed
- Write suggestions you can believe
- Imagine you are talking to a bright eight-year-old
- Focus on what you desire, not what you don't want.

The hell versus opportunity exercise

Now, let's start transforming those go-to negative limiting beliefs you identified above. Take a piece of paper and divide it into two columns. Name the first column 'Hell' (or if you prefer you can just say 'limiting beliefs') and write down the words you usually say to yourself when speaking about this particular challenge: "I am the worst speaker, I am incompetent, I am not good enough, I always botch up such and such".

Now, name the second column "Opportunity" and for every negative belief, come up with an alternative set of words that you can use to replace the first set. This is what your response is going to be when the negative thoughts emerge. Make sure you word your sentences in a way that makes you truly believe them. If necessary, use progressive words.

Remember, this is about choosing a better, more useful perspective, taking responsibility for change, and clearly telling your mind what you want (not what you don't want) with positive words, in the present. It's about telling your mind you can change regardless of your past.

i.e.

HELL: *I always forget the lyrics of my song.*

OPPORTUNITY: *My memory is perfect, words flow easily.*

HELL: I worry about making mistake.

OPPORTUNITY: *Creativity is more important than perfection.*

HELL: *I am distracted by people in the audience.*

OPPORTUNITY: *I focus on the song.*

HELL: *What if they think I am incompetent?*

OPPORTUNITY: *The audience is on my side. They want me to do well.*

HELL: I hate performing

OPPORTUNITY: *The more I perform, the better I become, and the more I love it.*

HELL

....

....

OPPORTUNITY

....

....

HELL

....

....

OPPORTUNITY

....

....

HELL

....

....

OPPORTUNITY

....

....

HELL

....

....

OPPORTUNITY

....

....

HELL

....

....

OPPORTUNITY

....

....

HELL

....

....

OPPORTUNITY

....

....

HELL

....

....

OPPORTUNITY

....

....

HELL

....

....

OPPORTUNITY

....

....

HELL

....

....

OPPORTUNITY

....

....

HELL

....

....

OPPORTUNITY

....

....

When you phrase your suggestions or affirmations, you can address yourself either in the first person, for example, "I am...." or in the second person, such as "You are..."

There are studies that suggest that using the second person can be more powerful, especially when used in conjunction with your given name. So, if your name is Kathy, you may write something like: "Kathy, you are a wonderful teacher!". However, I suggest you experiment and see what works best for you.

Here's a little sum up of how to flip those negative limiting beliefs:

1) **Straightforward flip**: just flip it to its opposite

ie.. I stumble on my words - My words flow out of me freely and easily

2) **Progressive**: if the gap between where you are and where you want to be seems just too big use a suggestion about a state that changes over time.

ie. the more I exercise the more I get fit the more I love exercising

3) **Coping** with a worst case catastrophic scenario

ie even if .... (worst case scenario) I can cope. (or I'll be ok)

Once you have this set of alternative statements, start challenging yourself. Use them in your daily life by either saying them aloud or internally, as thoughts.

How to use affirmations properly?

When:

If you decide to use affirmations, I would recommend you choose one belief that feels most relevant or a set of related beliefs at any one time. Repeat it to yourself, preferably before bed. This will help you go to sleep with a good frame of mind and allow for relaxation which, in turn, aids good sleep.

Another reason for repeating affirmations at night is that early morning REM phase dreaming helps grow new connections in the brain. Information acquired just before sleep is integrated especially well. If you repeat your affirmations in bed, you are helping to wire them deep into your system.

How:

The way to repeat the affirmations is also important. Don't just say them. Mean them. Imagine them. And most importantly, feel them. Remember, your subconscious responds to strong emotion. What would it be like to believe them to be true? What would it feel like if they were already a reality? Connect to the emotions you would feel. Choose to trust what you want is on its way.

How often:

The amount of repetition is also important. New habits are formed through repetition. I would suggest you repeat each affirmation to yourself slowly either aloud ten times, or silently twenty times. Saying something aloud makes it real and it is less likely you will be distracted by other thoughts, so if you choose to say the affirmations to yourself silently, you will need to repeat them more often.

The number of times I suggest here is not mandatory, but it is based both on the power of ritual and on ease of recall. Practicing silently before sleep may make you fall asleep, so if you choose to repeat them inwardly, I would suggest you count the times you are saying your affirmation using the fingers of both your hands. As you go through your hands twice you will have twenty affirmations done!

Repeating these phrases may feel unfamiliar, but stick with it. Initially, it will be a choice, something you decide to do. But eventually, it will start to become part of who you are. The more you practice this, the easier it will become, and the easier it becomes, the more you will want to do it. You are wiring your mind to move towards success instead of coming up with obstacles and resistances.

Other ways of using them:

Another way of using affirmations is to scatter them everywhere for you to see during the day. Here are some possibilities:

- You could create a reminder on your phone or turn them into a screensaver.
- You could pin them under your fridge magnet.
- You could write them on a card and put them in your wallet.

Your Commitment:

....

....

....

When I am going to practice my empowering beliefs

....

....

....

In what form / How ?

....

....

....

Remember to stop every time you see them and really connect to what they mean. Imagine how you'd feel if your affirmation was already a reality, and treat it as such.

If you write your affirmations on a card, always remember to bring it with you so that when you suddenly feel anxious or have a nagging negative thought, you can take the card out and say the affirmation aloud. This will snap you out of your current negative loop and help you switch on to a more helpful one that brings you closer to your goals and makes you feel good.

In this chapter we have learned how to use limiting beliefs to create empowering suggestions and affirmations you can use to transform your negative self talk and increase your confidence. In the next few chapters we are going to go through the ten sessions described in the book 'Dare to Be Seen' so either refer to part II, III and IV of the book or to module 1 of the online course titled 'No More Fear'. And now let's jump in and work on session 1 'Calming your body and mind'

4

Calming Your Body and Mind

Session One Homework

This chapter is in reference to Audio Session 1 “Calming the body and mind” You will find this either in part II of the “Dare to Be Seen” book (Audio Session 1) or in lesson 1, module 1 titled “No more fear” in the Dare to Be Seen Online course.

Practice diaphragmatic breathing for a minimum of five minutes every day for at least a week.

- Lie down with your legs and arms uncrossed or sit with a straight back, your feet flat on the floor and your hands by your side.
- Always breathe through your nose and keep your mouth closed.
- Remember to make your in-breaths shorter than your out-breaths: for example, if you breathe in you could count from one to four. When you breathe out, count to eight or more.

Make sure to fill in your belly, not just your chest.

Fill in the practice log and notice how listening to the audio and practicing diaphragmatic breathing makes a difference. What are you finding easy? What is more challenging? What stands in the way? Remember that every problems hides a gift. How can you best overcome the challenge? What do you notice changing as you stick to your routine?

MONDAY

Have you listened to your hypnotic audio?

....

If no, why not? What stood in the way?

....

....

....

How can you best overcome this challenge? What could you do differently?

....

....

....

If yes, what worked well for you? What benefits did you experience?

....

....

....

What else have you noticed?

....

....

....

Have you practiced your diaphragmatic breathing today? If so, for how long?

....

If no, why not? What stood in the way?

....

....

....

How can you best overcome this challenge? What could you do differently?

....

....

....

If yes, what worked well for you? What benefits did you experience?

....

....

....

What else have you noticed?

....

....

....

TUESDAY

Have you listened to your hypnotic audio?

....

If no, why not? What stood in the way?

....

....

....

How can you best overcome this challenge? What could you do differently?

....

....

....

If yes, what worked well for you? What benefits did you experience?

....

....

....

What else have you noticed?

....

....

....

Have you practiced your diaphragmatic breathing today? If so, for how long?

....

If no, why not? What stood in the way?

....

....

....

How can you best overcome this challenge? What could you do differently?

....

....

....

If yes, what worked well for you? What benefits did you experience?

....

....

....

What else have you noticed?

....

....

....

WEDNESDAY

Have you listened to your hypnotic audio?

....

If no, why not? What stood in the way?

....

....

....

How can you best overcome this challenge? What could you do differently?

....

....

....

If yes, what worked well for you? What benefits did you experience?

....

....

....

What else have you noticed?

....

....

....

Have you practiced your diaphragmatic breathing today? If so, for how long?

....

If no, why not? What stood in the way?

....

....

....

How can you best overcome this challenge? What could you do differently?

....

....

....

If yes, what worked well for you? What benefits did you experience?

....

....

....

What else have you noticed?

....

....

....

THURSDAY

Have you listened to your hypnotic audio?

....

If no, why not? What stood in the way?

....

....

....

How can you best overcome this challenge? What could you do differently?

....

....

....

If yes, what worked well for you? What benefits did you experience?

....

....

....

What else have you noticed?

....

....

....

Have you practiced your diaphragmatic breathing today? If so, for how long?

....

If no, why not? What stood in the way?

....

....

....

How can you best overcome this challenge? What could you do differently?

....

....

....

If yes, what worked well for you? What benefits did you experience?

....

....

....

What else have you noticed?

....

....

....

FRIDAY

Have you listened to your hypnotic audio?

....

If no, why not? What stood in the way?

....

....

....

How can you best overcome this challenge? What could you do differently?

....

....

....

If yes, what worked well for you? What benefits did you experience?

....

....

....

What else have you noticed?

....

....

....

Have you practiced your diaphragmatic breathing today? If so, for how long?

....

If no, why not? What stood in the way?

....

....

....

How can you best overcome this challenge? What could you do differently?

....

....

....

If yes, what worked well for you? What benefits did you experience?

....

....

....

What else have you noticed?

....

....

....

SATURDAY

Have you listened to your hypnotic audio?

....

If no, why not? What stood in the way?

....

....

....

How can you best overcome this challenge? What could you do differently?

....

....

....

If yes, what worked well for you? What benefits did you experience?

....

....

....

What else have you noticed?

....

....

....

Have you practiced your diaphragmatic breathing today? If so, for how long?

....

If no, why not? What stood in the way?

....

....

....

How can you best overcome this challenge? What could you do differently?

....

....

....

If yes, what worked well for you? What benefits did you experience?

....

....

....

What else have you noticed?

....

....

....

SUNDAY

Have you listened to your hypnotic audio?

....

If no, why not? What stood in the way?

....

....

....

How can you best overcome this challenge? What could you do differently?

....

....

....

If yes, what worked well for you? What benefits did you experience?

....

....

....

What else have you noticed?

....

....

....

Have you practiced your diaphragmatic breathing today? If so, for how long?

....

If no, why not? What stood in the way?

....

....

....

How can you best overcome this challenge? What could you do differently?

....

....

....

If yes, what worked well for you? What benefits did you experience?

....

....

....

What else have you noticed?

....

....

....

Check in

I have listened to this session ___ times.

Now that you have practiced listening to the hypnotic session several times let us cement the learning with some conscious exercises.

***

When you feel anxiety creep in, stop whatever you are doing, tap the side of your hand lightly and repeatedly.

Say out loud: "Even thought I am...(nervous, anxious, scared) I deeply and completely accept and love myself anyway."

Do this by tapping on the "karate chop point" of the hand. You can find out more about EFT by visiting https://www.elisadinapoli.com/EFT

Note down any reflections about how this practice has affected you. How effective has it been?

....

....

....

....

CHALLENGE

What is the biggest challenge that stands in your way to achieving the goals you set out in Guide 1? (Details of this are in the fb group Master The Stage)

....

....

....

....

....

....

What do you think you need to change in order to overcome it?

....

....

....

....

....

....

Share your insights with the Master The Stage FB Community!

(Post on Guide 3)

5

Connecting to Heart Wisdom

Session Two Homework

This chapter is in reference to Audio Session 2 "Connecting to heart wisdom". You will find this either in part II of the "Dare to Be Seen" book (Audio Session 2) or in lesson 2, module 1 titled "No more fear" in the Dare to Be Seen Online course.

In preparation for the upcoming hypnotic session number two, make sure you do the following exercises one after the other. Do not skip these, as they are essential to the success of the audio session.

Acceptance exercise

Think of a situation that makes you feel 'on the spot' – it could be an interview, an audition, giving a presentation or a speech, or performing in front of a crowd. Connect to your fear. On the dotted lines, write down what you fear:

For example:

I am scared that I will botch up the presentation because I'll be nervous. I am scared that I cannot stop my throat from drying up.

I am scared that...

I am worried that...

I can't do that because...

....

....

And that's okay

....

....

And that's okay

....

....

And that's okay

....

....

And that's okay

....

....

And that's okay

....

....

And that's okay

....

....

And that's okay

....

....

And that's okay

....

....

And that's okay

....

....

And that's okay

Notice how I have added 'and that's okay' to the end of these sentences. Once you have filled the left side, read out loud the sentences in full and notice what it is like to accept the idea that having fears is ok more fully. Record your reflections here:

....

....

....

....

....

....

....

....

....

....

Now listen to audio session two.

Check in

I have listened to this session ___ times.

Heart Connection

Once you have listened to audio session two, come back to this journal and copying the sentences from exercise one, fill in the rest with the 'deeper truth' you discovered during your session. If you only come up with a few, list them here, then go back to the hypnotic audio and work on each sentence until you have the 'deeper truth' for each one.

A part of me is worried that

....

....

....

But deep down my heart knows

....

....

....

A part of me is worried that

....

....

....

But deep down my heart knows

....

....

....

A part of me is worried that

....

....

....

But deep down my heart knows

....

....

....

A part of me is worried that

....

....

....

But deep down my heart knows

....

....

....

A part of me is worried that

....

....

....

But deep down my heart knows

....

....

....

A part of me is worried that

....

....

....

But deep down my heart knows

....

....

....

A part of me is worried that

....

....

....

But deep down my heart knows

....

....

....

A part of me is worried that

....

....

....

But deep down my heart knows

....

....

....

A part of me is worried that

....

....

....

But deep down my heart knows

....

....

....

A part of me is worried that

....

....

....

But deep down my heart knows

....

....

....

Read the sentences aloud to yourself. For example:

'A part of me is scared that I will blank out and forget my speech, but deep down my heart knows I don't have to be perfect. I can take a deep breath, take my time, and reconnect to the message.'

How does this make you feel?

....

....

....

....

....

....

You could now transfer your deeper truths and power statements to a piece of paper and carry it with you. Alternatively, you could set a reminder on your phone or create a screensaver on your computer. Be creative with this!

Whenever your negative feelings try to return, use your peaceful place anchor, breathe deeply, and remind yourself of your deeper truth by saying it out loud 3 to 5 times, really focussing on the meaning of the words and connecting to the positive feelings they elicit.

CHALLENGE

Share Your most important "Deeper Truth" with the MTS Community!

(guide 4)

6

Coping with Excessive Anxiety

Session Three Homework

This chapter is in reference to Audio Session 3 “Coping with excessive anxiety“. You will find this either in part II of the “Dare to Be Seen” book (Audio Session 3) or in lesson 3, module 1, titled “No more fear” in the Dare to Be Seen Online course.

To prepare for your audio session, create a list of scary situations. For example:

- *Being asked to make a speech of the spot*
- *Arranging a booking for a gig*
- *Playing a piece in front of an audition panel*
- *Pitching a project at a meeting.*

....

....

....

....

....

....

....

....

....

....

After brainstorming all the situations in which you imagine feeling scared or nervous, grade them on a scale of 1 to 10. One would be a situation that makes you only slightly nervous. Ten would be the most terrifying situation you could face. After grading them, put them in order from the least scary to the most frightening.

1..

2..

3..

4..

5..

6..

7..

8..

9..

10..

Start addressing the situation with the score of 1/10. Use this situation in your hypnotic recording. When you are done listening, ask yourself:

When you think of this situation now, how confident do you feel about coping with it, on a scale of 0 to 10?

....

How different do you feel now? Why? What has changed?

....

....

....

....

....

....

....

....

....

....

What was the most useful part of this session? Why?

....

....

....

....

....

....

Listen to audio recording two every day, until your level of confidence with the situation you have chosen has risen as close to 10 as possible. Then, engage in the same situation in the real world. When you have done so, reflect:

What is it like to engage in this situation now? What has changed? Why?

....

....

....

....

....

....

....

....

What worked well?

....

....

....

....

....

....

....

....

What is still challenging?

....

....

....

....

....

....

....

....

How can you best overcome this challenge?

....

....

....

....

....

....

....

....

Based on your discoveries, commit to one course of action that can help you overcome your challenge.

I commit to

....

....

....

When you feel you can cope well with it, move to the next situation on the list.

***

Start addressing the situation with the score of 2/10. Use this situation in your hypnotic recording. When you are done listening, ask yourself:

When you think of this situation now, how confident do you feel about coping with it, on a scale of 0 to 10?

....

How different do you feel now? Why? What has changed?

....

....

....

....

....

....

....

....

....

....

What was the most useful part of this session? Why?

....

....

....

....

....

....

Listen to audio recording two every day, until your level of confidence with the situation you have chosen has risen as close to 10 as possible. Then, engage in the same situation in the real world. When you have done so, reflect:

What is it like to engage in this situation now? What has changed? Why?

....

....

....

....

....

....

....

....

What worked well?

....

....

....

....

....

....

....

....

What is still challenging?

....

....

....

....

....

....

....

....

How can you best overcome this challenge?

....

....

....

....

....

....

....

....

Based on your discoveries, commit to one course of action that can help you overcome your challenge.

I commit to

....

....

....

When you feel you can cope well with it, move to the next situation on the list.

***

Start addressing the situation with the score of 3/10. Use this situation in your hypnotic recording. When you are done listening, ask yourself:

When you think of this situation now, how confident do you feel about coping with it, on a scale of 0 to 10?

....

How different do you feel now? Why? What has changed?

....

....

....

....

....

....

....

....

....

....

What was the most useful part of this session? Why?

....

....

....

....

....

....

Listen to audio recording two every day, until your level of confidence with the situation you have chosen has risen as close to 10 as possible. Then, engage in the same situation in the real world. When you have done so, reflect:

What is it like to engage in this situation now? What has changed? Why?

....

....

....

....

....

....

....

....

What worked well?

....

....

....

....

....

....

....

....

What is still challenging?

....

....

....

....

....

....

....

....

How can you best overcome this challenge?

....

....

....

....

....

....

....

....

Based on your discoveries, commit to one course of action that can help you overcome your challenge.

I commit to

....

....

....

When you feel you can cope well with it, move to the next situation on the list.

***

Start addressing the situation with the score of 4/10. Use this situation in your hypnotic recording. When you are done listening, ask yourself:

When you think of this situation now, how confident do you feel about coping with it, on a scale of 0 to 10?

....

How different do you feel now? Why? What has changed?

....

....

....

....

....

....

....

....

....

....

What was the most useful part of this session? Why?

....

....

....

....

....

....

Listen to audio recording two every day, until your level of confidence with the situation you have chosen has risen as close to 10 as possible. Then, engage in the same situation in the real world. When you have done so, reflect:

What is it like to engage in this situation now? What has changed? Why?

....

....

....

....

....

....

....

....

What worked well?

....

....

....

....

....

....

....

....

What is still challenging?

....

....

....

....

....

....

....

....

How can you best overcome this challenge?

....

....

....

....

....

....

....

....

Based on your discoveries, commit to one course of action that can help you overcome your challenge.

I commit to

....

....

....

When you feel you can cope well with it, move to the next situation on the list.

***

Start addressing the situation with the score of 5/10. Use this situation in your hypnotic recording. When you are done listening, ask yourself:

When you think of this situation now, how confident do you feel about coping with it, on a scale of 0 to 10?

....

How different do you feel now? Why? What has changed?

....

....

....

....

....

....

....

....

....

....

What was the most useful part of this session? Why?

....

....

....

....

....

....

Listen to audio recording two every day, until your level of confidence with the situation you have chosen has risen as close to 10 as possible. Then, engage in the same situation in the real world. When you have done so, reflect:

What is it like to engage in this situation now? What has changed? Why?

....

....

....

....

....

What worked well?

What is still challenging?

How can you best overcome this challenge?

....

....

....

....

....

....

....

....

Based on your discoveries, commit to one course of action that can help you overcome your challenge.

I commit to

....

....

....

When you feel you can cope well with it, move to the next situation on the list.

***

Start addressing the situation with the score of 6/10. Use this situation in your hypnotic recording. When you are done listening, ask yourself:

When you think of this situation now, how confident do you feel about coping with it, on a scale of 0 to 10?

....

How different do you feel now? Why? What has changed?

....

....

....

....

....

....

....

....

....

....

What was the most useful part of this session? Why?

....

....

....

....

....

....

Listen to audio recording two every day, until your level of confidence with the situation you have chosen has risen as close to 10 as possible. Then, engage in the same situation in the real world. When you have done so, reflect:

What is it like to engage in this situation now? What has changed? Why?

....

....

....

....

....

....

....

....

What worked well?

....

....

....

....

....

....

....

....

What is still challenging?

....

....

....

....

....

....

....

....

How can you best overcome this challenge?

....

....

....

....

....

....

....

....

Based on your discoveries, commit to one course of action that can help you overcome your challenge.

I commit to

....

....

....

When you feel you can cope well with it, move to the next situation on the list.

***

Start addressing the situation with the score of 7/10. Use this situation in your hypnotic recording. When you are done listening, ask yourself:

When you think of this situation now, how confident do you feel about coping with it, on a scale of 0 to 10?

....

How different do you feel now? Why? What has changed?

....

....

....

....

....

....

....

....

....

....

What was the most useful part of this session? Why?

....

....

....

....

....

....

Listen to audio recording two every day, until your level of confidence with the situation you have chosen has risen as close to 10 as possible. Then, engage in the same situation in the real world. When you have done so, reflect:

What is it like to engage in this situation now? What has changed? Why?

....

....

....

....

....

....

....

....

What worked well?

....

....

....

....

....

....

....

....

What is still challenging?

....

....

....

....

....

....

....

....

How can you best overcome this challenge?

....

....

....

....

....

....

....

....

Based on your discoveries, commit to one course of action that can help you overcome your challenge.

I commit to

....

....

....

When you feel you can cope well with it, move to the next situation on the list.

***

Start addressing the situation with the score of 8/10. Use this situation in your hypnotic recording. When you are done listening, ask yourself:

When you think of this situation now, how confident do you feel about coping with it, on a scale of 0 to 10?

....

How different do you feel now? Why? What has changed?

....

....

....

....

....

....

....

....

....

....

What was the most useful part of this session? Why?

....

....

....

....

....

....

Listen to audio recording two every day, until your level of confidence with the situation you have chosen has risen as close to 10 as possible. Then, engage in the same situation in the real world. When you have done so, reflect:

What is it like to engage in this situation now? What has changed? Why?

....

....

....

....

....

....

....

....

What worked well?

....

....

....

....

....

....

....

....

What is still challenging?

....

....

....

....

....

....

....

....

How can you best overcome this challenge?

....

....

....

....

....

....

....

....

Based on your discoveries, commit to one course of action that can help you overcome your challenge.

I commit to

....

....

....

When you feel you can cope well with it, move to the next situation on the list.

***

Start addressing the situation with the score of 9/10. Use this situation in your hypnotic recording. When you are done listening, ask yourself:

When you think of this situation now, how confident do you feel about coping with it, on a scale of 0 to 10?

....

How different do you feel now? Why? What has changed?

....

....

....

....

....

....

....

....

....

....

What was the most useful part of this session? Why?

....

....

....

....

....

....

Listen to audio recording two every day, until your level of confidence with the situation you have chosen has risen as close to 10 as possible. Then, engage in the same situation in the real world. When you have done so, reflect:

What is it like to engage in this situation now? What has changed? Why?

....

....

....

....

....

....

....

....

What worked well?

....

....

....

....

....

....

....

....

What is still challenging?

....

....

....

....

....

....

....

....

How can you best overcome this challenge?

....

....

....

....

....

....

....

....

Based on your discoveries, commit to one course of action that can help you overcome your challenge.

I commit to

....

....

....

When you feel you can cope well with it, move to the next situation on the list.

***

Start addressing the situation with the score of 10/10. Use this situation in your hypnotic recording. When you are done listening, ask yourself:

When you think of this situation now, how confident do you feel about coping with it, on a scale of 0 to 10?

....

How different do you feel now? Why? What has changed?

....

....

....

....

....

....

....

....

....

....

What was the most useful part of this session? Why?

....

....

....

....

....

....

Listen to audio recording two every day, until your level of confidence with the situation you have chosen has risen as close to 10 as possible. Then, engage in the same situation in the real world. When you have done so, reflect:

What is it like to engage in this situation now? What has changed? Why?

What worked well?

What is still challenging?

....

....

....

....

....

....

How can you best overcome this challenge?

....

....

....

....

....

....

....

....

Based on your discoveries, commit to one course of action that can help you overcome your challenge.

I commit to

....

....

....

CHALLENGE

After getting as close to a 10/10 in confidence level with an item of your choice on the list, challenge yourself to tackle that situation in real life.

My real life situation is

....

....

....

....

....

....

....

....

....

Here are my wins:

....

....

....

....

....

....

....

....

....

....

Now share them with the MTS Fb Community! (guide 5)

7

Letting Go of the Past

Session Four Homework

This chapter is in reference to Audio Session 4 "Letting go of the past". You will find this either in part III of the "Dare to Be Seen" book (Audio Session 4) or in lesson 1, module 2, titled "A better future" in the Dare to Be Seen Online course.

Listen to your recording for session four until you feel you have thoroughly let go of the past. It may be that once is enough, or you may need to repeat the process several times. Once that is done proceed with the following exercises:

Create a ritual around getting rid of your 'house of the past'

For example, you could draw a house on a piece of paper filled with objects and people that represent what you need to leave behind. Use colours that are meaningful to you and don't worry about being unable to draw. What is important is to connect with the symbols in the picture. Once you have drawn the house, get rid of it. You could literally burn the paper. You could bury it in your garden. You could draw a huge black cloud over it until you cannot see it anymore. If, on the other hand you possess an object that reminds you of a negative experience connected to your anxiety, choose to deliberately destroy it in a ritual fashion. Your mind works with metaphors, so follow your instincts and trust your creativity.

What have you chosen to use for this exercise?

How did it feel to get rid of the 'house of the past'?

Does this process feel complete? If not, what would make it so?

Create a symbol representing a new future you

Your subconscious responds to symbols, so create a symbol that represents the self-belief, the calm, the enjoyment, and the confidence that you want to bring into your performances. Take that symbol with you and draw power from it before every performance.

For example, you could draw a picture that represents your new confident self and put it in your pocket before you go on stage, touching it every time you need more confidence. Or, if there is a piece of music in your visualisation that makes you feel powerful and happy, listen to it before your performances. Or if you have a significant object, piece of jewellery, or piece of clothing that feels meaningfully connected to your hypnotic visualisation, wear it during your performances.

My symbol is

....

....

....

....

....

....

....

Look back at the present from the future

Imagine it's six months from now and you have achieved all of your performance goals. Look back over the past few months: what have you done that has made it possible for you to be here today? Stand up, get excited and talk about everything that has happened as if it was the best time of your life. Imagine you are telling your best friends about it. Time yourself and spend exactly five minutes doing this. Then write down this story below.

My story is

....

....

....

....

....

....

....

....

....

....

....

....

....

....

....

....

....

....

....

....

....

....

....

....

....

....

....

....

....

....

....

....

CHALLENGE

Which of the three possible homework exercises did you choose and why?

....

....

....

....

....

....

....

What were the results? What's your biggest takeaway?

....

....

....

....

....

....

....

....

....

Share with the MTS FB Community

(post on Guide 6)

8

Letting Go of What If

Session Five Homework

This chapter is in reference to Audio Session 5 "Letting go of what ifs'" You will find this either in part III of the "Dare to Be Seen" book (Audio Session 5) or in lesson 2, module 2, titled "A better future" in the Dare to Be Seen Online course.

It is now time to listen to your transformational hypnotic audio where you will learn how to deal with catastrophic thinking effectively. Make sure you repeat this session once a day for at least a week or until you begin to feel its effects.

Fill in the practice log and notice how listening to the audio makes a difference. What are you finding easy? What is more challenging? What stands in the way? Remember that every problems hides a gift. How can you best overcome the challenge? What do you notice changing as you stick to your routine?

MONDAY

Have you listened to your hypnotic audio?

....

If no, why not? What stood in the way?

....

....

....

....

....

....

How can you best overcome this challenge? What could you do differently?

....

....

....

....

....

....

If yes, what worked well for you? What benefits did you experience?

....

....

....

....

....

....

What else have you noticed?

....

....

....

....

....

....

TUESDAY

Have you listened to your hypnotic audio?

....

If no, why not? What stood in the way?

....

....

....

....

....

....

How can you best overcome this challenge? What could you do differently?

....

....

....

....

....

....

If yes, what worked well for you? What benefits did you experience?

....

....

....

....

....

....

What else have you noticed?

....

....

....

....

....

....

WEDNESDAY

Have you listened to your hypnotic audio?

....

If no, why not? What stood in the way?

How can you best overcome this challenge? What could you do differently?

If yes, what worked well for you? What benefits did you experience?

What else have you noticed?

....

....

....

....

....

....

THURSDAY

Have you listened to your hypnotic audio?

....

If no, why not? What stood in the way?

....

....

....

....

....

....

How can you best overcome this challenge? What could you do differently?

....

....

....

....

....

....

If yes, what worked well for you? What benefits did you experience?

....

....

....

....

....

....

What else have you noticed?

....

....

....

....

....

....

FRIDAY

Have you listened to your hypnotic audio?

....

If no, why not? What stood in the way?

....

....

....

....

....

....

How can you best overcome this challenge? What could you do differently?

....

....

....

....

....

....

If yes, what worked well for you? What benefits did you experience?

....

....

....

....

....

....

What else have you noticed?

....

....

....

....

....

....

SATURDAY

Have you listened to your hypnotic audio?

....

If no, why not? What stood in the way?

....

....

....

....

....

....

How can you best overcome this challenge? What could you do differently?

....

....

....

....

....

....

If yes, what worked well for you? What benefits did you experience?

....

....

....

....

....

....

What else have you noticed?

....

....

....

....

....

....

SUNDAY

Have you listened to your hypnotic audio?

....

If no, why not? What stood in the way?

....

....

....

....

....

....

How can you best overcome this challenge? What could you do differently?

....

....

....

....

....

....

If yes, what worked well for you? What benefits did you experience?

....

....

....

....

....

....

What else have you noticed?

....

....

....

....

....

....

Check in

I have listened to this session ___ times.

Now that you have practiced listening to the hypnotic session several times let us cement the learning with some conscious exercises.

***

If you find yourself overestimating the possibility that things will turn out badly, or if you often jump to worst case scenarios, you are probably looking at the world in a way that makes it seem more dangerous than it really is. It's as if you are wearing the opposite of rose-tinted glasses. Your glasses are like the distorting mirrors you find in amusement park horror houses. You see every negative thought as a fact. You assume you have little ability to cope with life's problems and you discredit your positive qualities.

These irrational, pessimistic attitudes are known as cognitive distortions. Have a look at the following list and complete the exercise outlined underneath it.

Cognitive Distortions

All or nothing thinking—Looking at things in black or white categories with no middle ground.

e.g. If I fall short of perfection, I am a total failure. Making mistakes means I am worthless.

Overgeneralisation—Generalising from a single negative experience and expecting it to hold true forever.

e.g. I got the presentation wrong. I'll never get it right. I botched up the interview. I'll never get the job I want.

Negative Bias—Focusing on the negative and filtering out all the positives. Only noticing the one thing that went wrong and ignoring all the things that went right.

e.g. It was a disaster,I played the wrong chord in the second verse of the song!

Discounting the Positive—Coming up with reasons why positive events don't count.

e.g. I got the part, but it was just luck.

Jumping to conclusions—Making negative interpretations without actual evidence as if you could read minds.

e.g. I could tell the audience hated it. Or, I just know something is going to go wrong.

Catastrophising—Expecting the worst-case scenario to happen.

e.g. Nobody is going to come to see the play. I am going to be so terrible at speaking, I will lose my job. They are going to think I am incompetent.

Emotional Reasoning—Believing the way you feel reflects reality.

e.g. I am really scared so I must be in danger. I feel worried I might fail, so I must be a failure.

Demanding—Holding yourself to a strict list of what you should and should not do and beating yourself up if you break your own rules.

e.g. I should be calm. I should play the piece without any mistakes. (If I don't, I don't deserve the job)

Labelling—Labelling yourself based on mistakes and perceived shortcomings. This is equivalent to putting yourself in a cage and throwing away the key.

e.g. I am a loser. I am an idiot. I am a failure. I am a mediocre speaker.

Personalisation—Assuming responsibility for things that are outside your control.

e.g. It's my fault the computer broke down in the middle of the presentation. I should have bought a better computer that doesn't break down.

Now that you are familiar with these cognitive distortions let's put your knowledge to the test:

1) **Write down your rendition of the worst possible performance-**, presentation, interview, audition, or speech you could ever give. Allow yourself to be honest about your fears, and just go for it without editing. When you are done, go through the list of cognitive errors listed before the audio and underline all the cognitive errors you notice in your writing.

For example:

- *My presentation will go as badly as last time. (Overgeneralisation)*
- *I will get my words wrong and it'll be a total disaster. (Black and white thinking)*
- *People will laugh and think I am a fraud. (Catastrophizing and jumping to conclusions)*
- *I am so incompetent and stupid. (Labelling)*

This is my worst possible case scenario:

....

....

....

....

....

....

....

....

....

....

....

....

....

When you have finished, use the objection technique to flip them around. (See chapter 3 and 5 of this journal for details)

Here are my cognitive errors:

....

....

....

....

....

....

....

Here are my 'flips'

....

....

....

....

....

....

....

....

....

....

....

....

....

....

....

....

....

....

....

....

2) **Rewrite your day using positive language.**

Exaggerate and emotionalise. Remember your subconscious is like a smart eight-year-old. Use big, exciting words and use the present tense.

For example:

I wake up refreshed after a good night's sleep. I put a song on that makes me feel good. I visualise the performance going well and tell myself I am excited about it. I go to work and feel good about the opportunity I have been given to share my knowledge or song with my audience... (Keep going.)

You could use this to create a bespoke session for yourself by recording it as an autosuggestion. For more information on how to do this, read chapter 2 of this journal or Chapter 6 and Bonus Session 3 of the Dare to be seen book.

Here is my 'new' experience on performance day:

....

....

....

....

....

What is the most common cognitive distortion you fall into on a regular basis?

What is its ‘flip’?

....

....

....

....

....

....

Share with the MTS FB Community!

(Post on Guide 7)

9

Letting Go of Worry

Session Six Homework

This chapter is in reference to Audio Session 6 "Letting go of what worry". You will find this either in part III of the "Dare to Be Seen" book (Audio Session 6) or in lesson 3, module 2, titled "A better future" in the Dare to Be Seen Online course.

My method to successfully deal with worry has two different components:

- *Using a strategy of postponing worry combined with problem solving to empower you to change what you can change and let go of what you cannot.*
- *Using hypnosis to construct metaphors that will help you let go of worry.*

The first strategy will be outlined in the homework for this session (see below, after practice log). The second will be used in the transformational hypnotic audio that you either have created using instructions from the Dare to Be Seen book or listening to the recording from the Dare to Be Seen Premium Online Course.

First, select a specific worry you have around performing and listen to your transformational hypnotic audio recording. Listen to this recording every time you want to let go of a specific worry.

Fill in the practice log and notice how listening to the audio makes a difference. What are you finding easy? What is more challenging? What stands in the way? Remember that every problems hides a gift. How can you best overcome the challenge? What do you notice changing as you stick to your routine?

MONDAY

Have you listened to your hypnotic audio?

....

If no, why not? What stood in the way?

....

....

....

....

....

....

How can you best overcome this challenge? What could you do differently?

....

....

....

....

....

....

If yes, what worked well for you? What benefits did you experience?

....

....

....

....

....

....

What else have you noticed?

....

....

....

....

....

....

TUESDAY

Have you listened to your hypnotic audio?

....

If no, why not? What stood in the way?

....

....

....

....

....

....

How can you best overcome this challenge? What could you do differently?

....

....

....

....

....

....

If yes, what worked well for you? What benefits did you experience?

....

....

....

....

....

....

What else have you noticed?

....

....

....

....

....

....

WEDNESDAY

Have you listened to your hypnotic audio?

....

If no, why not? What stood in the way?

....

....

....

....

....

....

How can you best overcome this challenge? What could you do differently?

....

....

....

....

....

....

If yes, what worked well for you? What benefits did you experience?

....

....

....

....

....

....

What else have you noticed?

....

....

....

....

....

....

THURSDAY

Have you listened to your hypnotic audio?

....

If no, why not? What stood in the way?

....

....

....

....

....

....

How can you best overcome this challenge? What could you do differently?

....

....

....

....

....

....

If yes, what worked well for you? What benefits did you experience?

....

....

....

....

....

....

What else have you noticed?

....

....

....

....

....

....

FRIDAY

Have you listened to your hypnotic audio?

....

If no, why not? What stood in the way?

....

....

....

....

....

....

How can you best overcome this challenge? What could you do differently?

....

....

....

....

....

....

If yes, what worked well for you? What benefits did you experience?

....

....

....

....

....

....

What else have you noticed?

....

....

....

....

....

....

SATURDAY

Have you listened to your hypnotic audio?

....

If no, why not? What stood in the way?

....

....

....

....

....

....

How can you best overcome this challenge? What could you do differently?

....

....

....

....

....

....

If yes, what worked well for you? What benefits did you experience?

....

....

....

....

....

....

What else have you noticed?

....

....

....

....

....

....

SUNDAY

Have you listened to your hypnotic audio?

....

If no, why not? What stood in the way?

....

....

....

....

....

....

How can you best overcome this challenge? What could you do differently?

....

If yes, what worked well for you? What benefits did you experience?

What else have you noticed?

Check in

I have listened to this session ___ times.

Now that you have practiced listening to the hypnotic session several times let us cement the learning with some conscious exercises.

***

After you've listened to your recording:

When you postpone worry, you are effectively breaking the habit of dwelling on worries so you can get on with what you want to do. You are not struggling to suppress your anxious thoughts. You are simply saving them for later.

So, rather than trying to cancel the worry, you are buying yourself a "moment of calm". In this moment, you have an opportunity to just be, because the part of you which wants to worry is satisfied, knowing you'll do it later. As you develop your ability to postpone the anxious thoughts and resolve problems that are within your control, you will discover that you have more influence than you think.

Sometimes, worrying feels good because when you run through a problem in your head, you are distracting yourself from the unpleasant emotions you may have about the event. It may also feel like you are accomplishing something. But worrying is very different from problem solving.

When you problem solve, you evaluate a situation and come up with concrete steps for dealing with it. You then put into practice your plan and take action. When you worry however, you rarely find solutions. Keeping this in mind, proceed with the following exercise.

<u>You will need:</u>

- A dedicated 'worry notebook'. (You can use this journal the first time you do this)
- A pen.
- Half an hour, every day, until you have mastered this technique.

1. **Create a "worry period"**. Choose a set time and place for worrying. It should be the same every day (e.g. in the living room from 5:00 to 5:20 p.m.) and early enough that it won't make you anxious right before bedtime. During your worry period, you're allowed to worry about whatever is on your mind. The rest of the day, however, is a worry-free zone.

When is your worry period?

....

....

....

2. **Postpone your worry**. If an anxious thought comes into your head during the day, make a brief note of it and then continue going about your day. Remind yourself that you'll have time to think about it later, so there's no need to worry about it right now.

3. **Go over your "worry list" during the worry period**. If the thoughts you wrote down are still bothering you, allow yourself to worry about them, but only for the amount of time allocated for your worry period. If they don't seem important any more, cut your worry period short and enjoy the rest of the day.

What to do during your worry period:

When the allotted time comes, open your worry book, and if you have any additional anxious thoughts about your performance, write them down. Identify the frightening thought. Be as detailed as possible about what you fear. Now, remember that these are not facts, but hypotheses that you are going to test. The idea is to challenge and examine these thoughts so you can develop a more balanced perspective.

Let's practice! These are the things I am worried might go wrong:

So, let's start by noticing if there are any cognitive errors present. You can find a list of cognitive errors in the previous chapter. Underline the text that represents a cognitive distortion.

Now ask these questions for each cognitive distortion, starting from the most disturbing one:

Is the problem something you are currently facing or is it an imaginary "what if"?

....

....

....

If it is a 'what if?' what's the probability on a scale of 0 to 10 that it will happen?

....

....

....

If the probability is low, what are some more likely outcomes?

....

....

....

....

....

....

What is a more positive and realistic way of looking at the situation?

....

....

....

....

....

....

....

....

....

Is the thought you are looking at absolutely 100% true beyond any shadow of a doubt?

....

....

....

....

....

....

....

Is the thought helpful?

....

....

....

....

....

How will worrying about this help you? How will it hurt you?

....

....

....

....

....

What would you say to a friend who had this worry?

....

....

....

....

....

....

Can you do something about the problem or is it out of your control?

....

....

....

....

....

....

....

Choose another cognitive distortion and repeat the exercise until you have examined all of them.

Once you have finished, reflect on how many of the worries you have listed are about issues that you cannot do anything about.

For example: People might not like the performance. Make a note of them and list them below.

Option 1: Things I cannot change / out of my control

....

....

....

....

....

....

....

....

....

....

....

....

....

....

Once you have finished, reflect on how many of the worries you have listed are about issues that you can do something about. For example: I am afraid I might not be prepared enough. Make a note of them and list them below.

Option 2: Things I can change / in my control

....

....

....

....

....

....

....

Now let's deal with option 1. If the worry is about a problem you cannot solve, you need to tune into your emotions. Worrying helps you avoid unpleasant emotions by keeping you in your head. When you are in your head, you don't feel what's going on underneath. Although they will be temporarily suppressed while you worry, as soon as you stop, your negative feelings will return. Then you may start to worry about them: "What's wrong with me? I shouldn't feel this way!"

To stop this vicious cycle, you need to embrace how you feel. If this is scary to you, it may be because you believe you should always be rational and in control. Or because you think your feelings should always make sense. Or because you think certain emotions are not appropriate, such as fear or anger.

Try to accept that emotions, like life, don't always make sense. They are not always pleasant, but they are part of being a human. Let yourself experience them and trust that all that is needed is for them to be expressed.

Like water in a river, emotions need to flow. Trust that when you let yourself express even the most unpleasant of emotions, they will eventually become different and more manageable. Nothing lasts forever, and feelings shift and change like water. So, try to accept the items in the right-hand column and allow full expression of the feelings that emerge when you do.

As you observe them, imagine you are an outsider looking in. You are not reacting to or judging your feelings. Instead, you treat them like stormy clouds carrying heavy rain. You watch the storm come, and eventually pass. You are like a mountain, witnessing the weather without becoming stuck on a set of conditions. You don’t engage; you observe instead, because it’s only when you engage and hold on that you get stuck.

Let us now look at option 2. If the worry is about a problem you can solve, now is the time to start brainstorming. Look at what you wrote in the section that says ’Option 2’ and make a list of all the possible solutions you can think of. Go in order. Don’t become too hung up on finding the perfect solution. Focus on what you have the power to change.

Here are the possible solutions I can think of:

....

....

....

....

....

....

....

....

....

....

....

....

....

....

....

....

....

....

....

....

When you have finished brainstorming, pick the first item and ask yourself:

What first small step can I take in the right direction?

....

....

....

....

....

....

Take action immediately. Once you have a plan and start doing something about the problem, you will feel a lot less worried. When you are done with this problem, move on to the next item on the list. When half an hour has passed, stop working; the rest can wait until tomorrow.

CHALLENGE

Choose a worry you can do something about.

My worry is

....

....

....

....

....

....

What is the first step you can take today that will take you towards a possible solution?

....

....

....

....

....

....

Take that step and share the result with the MTS FB Group so you can inspire others to do the same!

(Post on Guide 8)

10

Being Present

Session Seven Homework

This chapter is in reference to Audio Session 7 "Being present". You will find this either in part III of the "Dare to Be Seen" book (Audio Session 7) or in lesson 4, module 2, titled "A better future" in the Dare to Be Seen Online course.

Fill in the practice log and notice how listening to the audio makes a difference. What are you finding easy? What is more challenging? What stands in the way? Remember that every problems hides a gift. How can you best overcome the challenge? What do you notice changing as you stick to your routine?

MONDAY

Have you listened to your hypnotic audio?

....

If no, why not? What stood in the way?

....

....

....

....

....

....

How can you best overcome this challenge? What could you do differently?

If yes, what worked well for you? What benefits did you experience?

What else have you noticed?

....

TUESDAY

Have you listened to your hypnotic audio?

....

If no, why not? What stood in the way?

....

....

....

....

....

....

How can you best overcome this challenge? What could you do differently?

....

....

....

....

....

....

If yes, what worked well for you? What benefits did you experience?

....

....

....

....

....

....

What else have you noticed?

....

....

....

....

....

....

WEDNESDAY

Have you listened to your hypnotic audio?

....

If no, why not? What stood in the way?

....

....

....

....

....

....

How can you best overcome this challenge? What could you do differently?

....

....

....

....

....

....

If yes, what worked well for you? What benefits did you experience?

....

....

....

....

....

....

What else have you noticed?

....

....

....

....

....

....

THURSDAY

Have you listened to your hypnotic audio?

....

If no, why not? What stood in the way?

....

....

....

....

....

....

How can you best overcome this challenge? What could you do differently?

....

....

....

....

....

....

If yes, what worked well for you? What benefits did you experience?

....

....

....

....

....

....

What else have you noticed?

....

....

....

....

....

....

FRIDAY

Have you listened to your hypnotic audio?

....

If no, why not? What stood in the way?

....

....

....

....

....

....

How can you best overcome this challenge? What could you do differently?

....

....

....

....

....

....

If yes, what worked well for you? What benefits did you experience?

....

....

....

....

....

....

What else have you noticed?

....

....

....

....

....

....

SATURDAY

Have you listened to your hypnotic audio?

....

If no, why not? What stood in the way?

....

....

....

....

....

....

How can you best overcome this challenge? What could you do differently?

....

....

....

....

....

....

If yes, what worked well for you? What benefits did you experience?

....

....

....

....

....

....

What else have you noticed?

....

....

....

....

....

....

SUNDAY

Have you listened to your hypnotic audio?

If no, why not? What stood in the way?

How can you best overcome this challenge? What could you do differently?

If yes, what worked well for you? What benefits did you experience?

....

....

What else have you noticed?

....

....

....

....

....

....

Check in

I have listened to this session ___ times.

Now that you have practiced listening to the hypnotic session several times let us cement the learning with some conscious exercises.

Getting back to the here and now

If you live in the past you will suffer from depression. If you live in the future you will experience anxiety. The truth is both the past and the future are illusions. They are concepts, not reality. The only reality that exists for sure is the present moment. Our thoughts can take us away from the present. If we give them energy and we get carried away, we get disconnected from the present. One way to get back to the here and now is to connect to your body. Here are some easy ways of doing that:

- *Sit still with your feet on the ground and your hands by your side. Try not to slouch. Pay attention to your breath for 10 minutes.*

- *Put on your favourite song and dance or sing or both!*
- *Play your favourite instrument. Don't worry about performance. Focus on the sound.*
- *Do any kind of physical activity that requires your full attention (i.e. rock climbing, football, tennis etc)*
- *Go for a walk in nature alone. Leave your phone at home. Listen to the sounds of nature and try to notice different types of plants, smells, colours and sounds.*
- *Bake or cook your favourite food or try a new recipe.*
- *Choose an everyday object. Write about it using sensory language (sight, smell, sound, taste). Stay away from feeling and thought, only focus on the object and its characteristics.*
- *Make art for yourself only. Don't worry about whether what you do makes sense or not. Let your hands do the work for you.*

These are just examples of what you could do. Be creative, there are no limits here.

When I am in my 'head' and I catch myself thinking about the past or the future I will

....

....

....

....

....

....

***

The best way to kick a bad habit is to replace it with a better one. The idea is to tell yourself you are already feeling the way you want to feel. When you engage in positive self-talk, you automatically remove all negative thoughts without trying. This feels unfamiliar at first, but as you keep repeating it and commit to make the unfamiliar familiar, it will change from something you do to who you are.

After you have listened to your hypnotic recording, practice using the empowering beliefs you worked on chapter 3. Alternatively, below are some affirmations that you can use to train your positive self-talk. Choose the ones that most resonate with you or make up new ones. Feel free to modify them and personalise them. Even if you haven't worked on flipping your limiting beliefs yet I strongly suggest you make up your own affirmations specific to your situation.

Here are my empowering beliefs:

....

....

....

....

....

....

....

....

....

....

....

....

....

....

....

....

....

....

....

....

....

The following are general anti-anxiety affirmations.

- *The calmer I feel, the more I make wise choices.*
- *I am in charge of what thoughts I choose to pay attention to and this gives me control over how I feel.*
- *I am in control of how I react to situations that frighten me.*
- *I choose to imagine how I want to behave in any given situation.*
- *I expect the best and accept the rest.*
- *I focus on the present, one minute at a time.*
- *I create the future by focusing on the present as I want it to be.*
- *I choose the emotions that I want in the present moment: calm, collected, and confident.*
- *When I feel I am stressing myself out, I choose to calm myself instead.*
- *I remember I am in control of how I respond to situations that trigger me.*
- *When I feel afraid, I imagine how I want to behave in the situation I fear.*
- *I focus on the road instead of the wall. I focus on what I want.*
- *I remember that no matter what may or may not happen, I can deal with it and I will survive.*
- *No matter what happens, I'll be ok.*
- *When I feel tension, I take a moment to take a deep breath and relax.*
- *I relax into existence.*
- *I choose to find the serenity to accept the things I cannot change, the courage to change the things I can, and the wisdom to know the difference.*
- *I focus on the present.*
- *I choose to feel grateful for all the good things I already have in my life.*

- *When I feel anxious, I stop myself from flying into the future.*
- *I bring myself back to the present, noticing all the good things that are already in my life.*
- *I stop feeding my worries. I focus on creating what I want.*
- *I cross that bridge if and when I get there.*
- *I change what I can and I let go of the rest.*
- *No matter what happens, I can deal with it.*
- *I can and I will.*
- *I am master of my fate and captain of my soul.*

Underline one 'master affirmation' or modify one you resonate with to make it fit with you. Repeat this to yourself several times a day.

My master affirmation is:

....

....

....

Dedicate ten minutes at a set time in the day to work on the rest of your affirmations. Whether you use the general anti-anxiety affirmations provided or your own, repeat them aloud to yourself and remember to really mean them and embody them. One idea is to repeat them before going to bed or just as you wake up every single day for at least five times each. Make a habit of it. A good way to do this is to attach this practice to something you already do daily (such as washing your teeth) or to set a daily alarm.

Alternatively, you could use them as suggestions by recording an induction (see Chapter 6 of the "Dare to Be Seen" book for instructions) followed by your chosen statements. Experiment with second person versus first person, for example: 'the calmer I feel...' or 'the calmer you feel...' Some people respond better to one or the other. Include your name when possible.

You could also use your favourite affirmations as phone reminders so they pop up at regular intervals throughout the day. Alternatively, write them down on a piece of paper you always carry with you or use them as a screensaver. Be creative.

The important thing is to remind your subconscious that this is your new way of thinking. Keep going for a minimum of 7 days or more until they stick, keeping in mind that you are combating a lifetime of negative self-talk, so don't give up until you feel they are working!

CHALLENGE

How have you chosen to use your master affirmation?

....

....

....

....

How much time have you spent practicing it?

....

....

....

....

Is that enough time or do you need more?

....

....

....

....

How has it changed your perspective?

....

....

....

....

Share it with the MTS FB Community!

(Post on guide 9)

11

Stopping Negative Thoughts

Session Eight Homework

This chapter is in reference to Audio Session 8 “Stopping negative thoughts“. You will find this either in part III of the “Dare to Be Seen” book (Audio Session 8) or in lesson 1, module 3, titled “Lasting Success“ in the Dare to Be Seen Online course.

Before you listen to your recording choose a situation in which you feel particularly anxious with regards to being in the public eye. Perhaps it’s the moment you step on the stage or the podium. Perhaps it’s the moment you sit down for your interview or audition. Perhaps the time you start your presentation.

Keeping this in mind, prepare to listen to your transformational hypnotic audio recording .

Check in

I have listened to this session ___ times.

***

Now that you have practiced listening to the hypnotic session several times let us cement the learning with some conscious exercises.

Ask yourself these questions:

What would you say are your strengths when it comes to performing?

....

....

....

....

....

....

....

....

....

....

What have other people said in the past you are good at?

....

....

....

....

....

....

....

....

....

....

How often do you specifically think of these strengths daily?

Write down the answers and make a list of your positive beliefs around performing. When you are done, ask yourself:

Which belief is going to help me move forward the most?

Which is the most empowering?

....

....

....

....

....

....

....

....

....

Select the most empowering belief and use it as your main affirmation. Is this different from the 'master affirmation' you used in chapter 10? What does that tell you?

....

....

....

....

Take Action! Find opportunities to remind yourself of your strengths during your next performance, interview, audition, speech, or presentation. Repeat your empowering belief to yourself several times before your performance and if need be, during it as well.

What do you notice when you use these affirmations regularly? How do they influence the way you feel about yourself and your 'performances'?

....

....

....

....

....

....

....

CHALLENGE

Share your experience of your latest 'performance', having used mental repetition to help you remind you of your strengths.

Share it with the MTS FB Community!

(Post on Guide 10)

12

From Self-Consciousness to Flow

Session Nine Homework

This chapter is in reference to Audio Session 9 "From self consciousness to flow". You will find this either in part III of the "Dare to Be Seen" book (Audio Session 9) or in lesson 2, module 4, titled "Lasting Success" in the Dare to Be Seen Online course.

In this session, you will learn how to get back into flow when you become momentarily self-conscious. Knowing how to deal with this common setback relieves the anxiety around it, helping you to feel more relaxed under pressure as well as making it a rarer occurrence.

Keeping this in mind, prepare to listen to your transformational hypnotic audio recording .

Check in

I have listened to this session ___ times.

***

After you have listened to your transformational hypnotic audio recording, it is time to reinforce the learning from this session.

Action Point:

Film yourself on your phone rehearsing giving a presentation or a speech, answering questions to an imaginary interview or playing a song. Look directly at the camera when you can. If you become self conscious at any stage simply acknowledge it and get back into flow. Do not stop the film. Afterwards watch yourself and notice all the things you did well first.

These are the things I did well in my 1st Practice:

....

....

....

....

....

....

....

....

....

Then notice what you can improve.

These are the things I could work to improve from my 1st Practice:

....

....

....

....

....

....

....

....

....

....

My confidence score after this practice session is: ___ out of 10.

Repeat the process a few times trying to implement any changes you deem necessary. Do not judge yourself. Practice compassion and focus on improvements. Notice how quickly you get better.

These are the things I did well in my 2nd Practice:

....

....

....

....

....

....

....

....

....

Then notice what you can improve.

These are the things I could work to improve from my 2nd Practice:

....

....

....

....

....

....

....

....

....

....

My confidence score after this practice session is: ___ out of 10.

Repeat the process a few times trying to implement any changes you deem necessary. Do not judge yourself. Practice compassion and focus on improvements. Notice how quickly you get better.

These are the things I did well in my 3rd Practice:

....

....

....

....

....

....

....

....

....

Then notice what you can improve.

These are the things I could work to improve from my 3rd Practice:

....

....

....

....

....

....

....

....

....

....

My confidence score after this practice session is: ___ out of 10.

Repeat the process a few times trying to implement any changes you deem necessary. Do not judge yourself. Practice compassion and focus on improvements. Notice how quickly you get better.

These are the things I did well in my 4th Practice:

....

....

....

....

....

....

....

....

....

Then notice what you can improve.

These are the things I could work to improve from my 4th Practice:

....

....

....

....

....

....

....

....

....

....

My confidence score after this practice session is: ___ out of 10.

Repeat the process a few times trying to implement any changes you deem necessary. Do not judge yourself. Practice compassion and focus on improvements. Notice how quickly you get better.

These are the things I did well in my 5th Practice:

....

....

....

....

....

....

....

....

....

Then notice what you can improve.

These are the things I could work to improve from my 5th Practice:

....

....

....

....

....

....

....

....

....

....

My confidence score after this practice session is: ___ out of 10.

Repeat the process a few times trying to implement any changes you deem necessary. Do not judge yourself. Practice compassion and focus on improvements. Notice how quickly you get better. .

These are the things I did well in my 6th Practice:

....

....

....

....

....

....

....

....

....

Then notice what you can improve.

These are the things I could work to improve from my 6th Practice:

....

....

....

....

....

....

....

....

....

....

My confidence score after this practice session is: ___ out of 10.

Repeat the process a few times trying to implement any changes you deem necessary. Do not judge yourself. Practice compassion and focus on improvements. Notice how quickly you get better.

These are the things I did well in my 7th Practice:

....

....

....

....

....

....

....

....

....

Then notice what you can improve.

These are the things I could work to improve from my 7th Practice:

....

....

....

....

....

....

....

....

....

....

My confidence score after this practice session is: ___ out of 10.

Repeat the process a few times trying to implement any changes you deem necessary. Do not judge yourself. Practice compassion and focus on improvements. Notice how quickly you get better.

These are the things I did well in my 8th Practice:

....

....

....

....

....

....

....

....

....

Then notice what you can improve.

These are the things I could work to improve from my 8th Practice:

....

....

....

....

....

....

....

....

....

....

My confidence score after this practice session is: ___ out of 10.

Repeat the process a few times trying to implement any changes you deem necessary. Do not judge yourself. Practice compassion and focus on improvements. Notice how quickly you get better.

These are the things I did well in my 9th Practice:

....

....

....

....

....

....

....

....

....

Then notice what you can improve.

These are the things I could work to improve from my 9th Practice:

....

....

....

....

....

....

....

....

....

....

My confidence score after this practice session is: ___ out of 10.

Repeat the process a few times trying to implement any changes you deem necessary. Do not judge yourself. Practice compassion and focus on improvements. Notice how quickly you get better.

These are the things I did well in my 10th Practice:

....

....

....

....

....

....

....

....

....

Then notice what you can improve.

These are the things I could work to improve from my 10th Practice:

....

....

....

....

....

....

....

....

....

....

My confidence score after this practice session is: ___ out of 10.

Now go back to your first practice. Notice the confidence score you gave yourself and how it compares with the confidence score from your 10th session.

Before I practiced my confidence was ___ out of 10. After 10 practice sessions my confidence is ___ out of 10.

Give yourself a pat on the back for all the good work you have done and reward yourself with something you really enjoy.

CHALLENGE

Share your latest video footage from the homework section of this session with the MTS FB Community and encourage one other with positive constructive feedback!

(Post it on Guide11)

13

Increasing Confidence

Session Ten Homework

This chapter is in reference to Audio Session 10 "Increasing Confidence" You will find this either in part III of the "Dare to Be Seen" book (Audio Session 10) or in lesson 3, module 4, titled "Lasting Success" in the Dare to Be Seen Online course.

Now it's time to really ramp up your confidence. In this last session, we are going to use anchors to help you release tension and feel really good about going on stage, giving that speech, or doing that interview. If you need a reminder of what an anchor is, please refer to Audio Session 1 in the online course.

Check in

I have listened to this session ___ times.

After you have listened to your transformational hypnotic audio remember to practice your anchors daily in and out of hypnosis. The more you do, the more powerful and effective the connection will be.

***

We learn by imitation. Others have trodden similar paths before, and as humans, we all have the same potential for growing and honing our skills. Modelling others is one the fastest ways of accessing parts of ourselves that are present within us in embryonic form. Modelling is different from copying.

You possess the same qualities you admire in others. If you didn't, you could not recognise them in anybody else.

Remember these people are not superhuman. They are just like you and me. At some point, they didn't have a clue what they were doing, but they committed to refining their craft and they became good at it. Talent is overrated; effort is a much bigger predictor of success. Let's get the process started right now.

1) **Begin by identifying someone in your field that you admire** for the qualities they possess. Perhaps they are excellent speakers, singers, musicians, actors, or presenters.

My role model is

....

....

2) **Make a list of the qualities they possess.** Be as specific as possible and describe in detail how you know they have those qualities. You could ask yourself questions such as:

How do they move their body?

....

....

....

....

....

....

....

....

How do they use their voice?

....

....

....

....

....

....

....

....

What thoughts do you imagine they have?

....

....

....

....

....

....

....

....

What do you imagine they would be saying to themselves as they step into the limelight?

....

....

....

....

....

....

....

....

What do you imagine they would be saying to themselves when they make a mistake?

....

....

....

....

....

....

....

....

....

How do you think they would handle failure?

....

....

....

....

....

....

....

....

3) **Now, the next time you are faced with a situation around performing in which you feel nervous, stop for a moment, and ask yourself:**

How would (the person I admire) handle this?

....

....

....

....

....

....

....

....

....

What would they do?

....

....

....

....

....

....

....

....

What would they say to themselves?

....

....

....

....

....

....

....

....

4) **Pretend you are that person, and experiment acting the way they would.** You may be surprised to find you can access resources you never knew you had inside yourself. Like an actor stepping into his or her character's shoes, you may find those very qualities you admired in them being awakened in yourself.

THE FINAL CHALLENGE

- Go live on the Master The Stage FB Group and either:

- Share your biggest challenges during this course and how you've overcome them.
- Share some advice you'd give to a newbie on the course
- Celebrate your Biggest Wins
- Give a 2 minute presentation about a topic you know a lot about
- Sing a song or play an instrument

(The video must be at least 2 minutes long and must be LIVE- no recorded videos!!)

Please note: everybody who does this goes in to **WIN a FREE COACHING SESSION!** (just email me to let me know you have done it including a link to your video)

14

About the Author

Elisa Di Napoli has been a full time integrative clinical hypnotherapist and coach since 2001, her practice expanding across New Zealand and Scotland. Her work places a great deal of importance on positive mental health, Neurolinguistic Psychology, and Holistic Coaching. She originally studied philosophy and comparative religion, but took on hypnotherapy and coaching after an interest in shamanism led her to explore the mind-body connection within altered states of consciousness.

She studied hypnotherapy at the prestigious Hypnotherapy Training Institute of Northern California, training with world-renowned teachers Randal Churchill and Ormond McGill. She also studied cognitive behaviour hypnotherapy and hypnotic coaching at the Anglo European College of Therapeutic Hypnosis.

Coming from a diverse background including philosophy, art, comparative religion, music performance and acting, she has a Graduate Diploma in Electronic Music Composition and Performance as well as BA(Hons) in Comparative Religion at the University of London. She is multi-instrumentalist and an accomplished singer-songwriter with 20 years of performance experience and eleven albums under her belt.

She is passionate about learning and has been involved in many drumming groups, improv comedy classes, performance workshops, drama and clowning classes. When she is not making music, writing fiction, talking on podcasts, delivering workshops or taking courses, she greatly enjoys the company of her kittens, Pallino Pavarotti and Indie Jones.

For more info:

Coaching: www.elisadinapoli.com

Music: www.elyssavulpes.com

DOWNLOAD the Dare to Be Seen BONUS PACKAGE

including a

FREE AUDIOBOOK and ONLINE COURSE

Templates, Training, Hypnosis Sessions and Resources to Kickstart your Journey into Authentic Confidence under the Spotlight!

TO DOWNLOAD GO TO

https://elisadinapoli.com/bonuses

Use your camera phone to open link

Made in the USA
Monee, IL
20 March 2024